THE
PYTHON BIBLE

VOLUME THREE
DATA SCIENCE

BY

FLORIAN DEDOV

TABLE OF CONTENT

INTRODUCTION

In our modern time, the amount of data grows exponentially. Over time, we learn to extract important information out of this data by analyzing it. The field which is primarily focusing on exactly that is called *data science*. We use data science to analyze share prices, the weather, demographics or to create powerful artificial intelligences. Every modern and big system has to deal with tremendous amounts of data that need to be managed and analyzed intelligently.

Therefore, it is more than reasonable to educate yourself in this area as much as possible. Otherwise you might get overrun by this fast-growing trend instead of being part of it.

THIS BOOK

If you have read the first two volumes of this series, you are already a decent Python programmer. You are able to develop complex scripts using advanced techniques like multithreading or network programming. A lot of these skills will be needed for this volume, since it's going to be quite complex and detailed.

Now in this volume, we are going to start by talking about the major libraries or modules for data science in Python. We are taking a look at advanced arrays and lists, professional data visualization, statistical analysis and advanced data science with data frames. At the end, you will be able to prepare, analyze and visualize your own big data sets. This will lay the foundations for future volumes about machine learning and finance.

This book is again full of new and more complex information. There is a lot to learn here so stay tuned and code along while reading. This will help you to understand the material better and to practice implementing it. I wish you a lot of fun and success with your journey and this book!

Just one little thing before we start. This book was written for you, so that you can get as much value as possible and learn to code effectively. If you find this book valuable or you think you have learned something new, please write a quick review on Amazon. It is completely free and takes about one minute. But it helps me produce more high quality books, which you can benefit from.

Thank you!

If you are interested in free educational content about programming and machine learning, check out: https://www.neuralnine.com/

1 – WHAT IS DATA SCIENCE?

Now before we do anything at all, we need to first define what we are even talking about when using the term *data science*. What is data science?

When we are dealing with data science or data analysis, we are always trying to generate or extract knowledge from our data. For this, we use models, techniques and theories from the areas of mathematics, statistics, computer science, machine learning and many more.

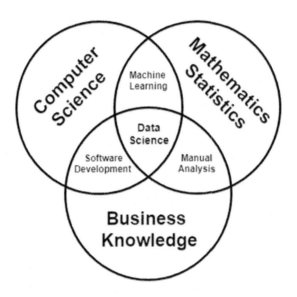

The figure above illustrates pretty accurately what data science actually is. When you combine computer science and business knowledge, you get software development and create business applications. When you combine your business knowledge with mathematics and statistics, you can also analyze the data but you have to do it manually, since you are missing the computational component. When you only combine computer science and statistics, you get machine learning, which is very powerful, but without the necessary business knowledge, you won't get any significant information or conclusions. We need to combine all of these three areas, in order to end up with data science.

However, in this volume we are not going to focus too much on the mathematics and the statistics or the machine learning algorithms. This will be the topic of future volumes. In this book we are focusing on the structuring, visualization and analyzing of the data.

WHY PYTHON?

Now, you should already know why Python is a good choice and a good programming language to learn. But why should we use it for data science? Aren't there better alternatives?

And although I hate polarizing answers and generalization, I have to bluntly say **NO!** You have some alternatives like the programming language *R* or *MATLAB* but they are not as big, as powerful and as simple as Python.

One of the main reasons for Python's popularity in this area is the large amount of libraries and modules for data science but also machine learning and scientific computing. We already have professional open-source libraries for managing lists, linear algebra, data visualization, machine learning, neural networks and much more.

Also, alternatives like R or MATLAB are very specialized in one single area like statistics or mathematical programming. Python on the other hand is a general-purpose language. We use it to code network scripts, video games, professional web applications, artificial intelligences and much more. Self-driving cars use Python, professional modelling software uses Python and also Pinterest was developed with Django, which is a Python framework.

For these reasons, Python has become one of the most popular programming languages out there, especially for machine learning and data science.

2 – INSTALLING MODULES

So the last thing we need to talk about before we get into the coding itself is the modules or libraries that we are going to use.

The following figure illustrates the structure of the modules that are used for data science and scientific computing.

As you can see, we have four major modules here and they all build on core Python. Basically, this is the hierarchy of these modules. *NumPy* builds on Python, *Matplotlib* uses or builds on *NumPy* and

Pandas builds on top of that. Of course there are other libraries that then build on top of *Pandas* as well. But for now, these are the modules that interest us.

Now in order to clear up the confusion, let's look at the purpose and functionalities of the individual libraries.

NUMPY

The *NumPy* module allows us to efficiently work with vectors, matrices and multi-dimensional arrays. It is crucial for linear algebra and numerical analysis. Also, it offers some advanced things like Fourier transforms and random number generation. It basically replaces the primitive and inefficient Python *list* with very powerful *NumPy arrays*.

Another thing worth mentioning is that NumPy was built in the *C* programming language. This means that it is a lot faster and more efficient than other Python libraries.

SCIPY

SciPy is a module which we are actually not going to use in this book. Nevertheless, it is worth mentioning because it is a very powerful library for scientific computing (maybe there will be a future volume about this).

However, SciPy can be seen as the application of NumPy to real problems. NumPy is basically just managing the arrays and lists. It is responsible for the operations like indexing, sorting, slicing, reshaping and so on. Now, SciPy actually uses NumPy to offer more abstract classes and functions that solve scientific problems. It gets deeper into the mathematics and adds substantial capabilities to NumPy.

MATPLOTLIB

On top of that, we have *Matplotlib*. This library is responsible for plotting graphs and visualizing our data. It offers numerous types of plotting, styles and graphs.

Visualization is a key step in data science. When we see our data in form of a graph, we can extract information and spot relations much easier. With Matplotlib we can do this professionally and very easy.

PANDAS

Last but not least, we have *Pandas*. This is the most high-level of our libraries and it builds on top of them. It offers us a powerful data structure named *data frame*. You can imagine it to be a bit like a mix of an Excel table and an SQL database table.

This library allows us to efficiently work with our huge amounts of interrelated data. We can merge, reshape, filter and query our data. We can iterate over it and we can read and write into files like CSV, XLSX and more. Also, it is very powerful when we work with databases, due to the similar structure of the tables.

Pandas is highly compatible with NumPy and Matplotlib, since it builds on them. We can easily convert data from one format to the other.

INSTALLING MODULES WITH PIP

Since all these modules don't belong to core Python, we will need to install them externally. For this, we are going to use *pip*. This is a recursive name and stands for *pip installs packages*.

In order to use pip, we just need to open up our terminal or command line. On windows this is CMD and on Mac and Linux it is the terminal. We then just use the following syntax, in order to install the individual packages.

```
pip install <package-name>
```

So what we need to do is to execute the following commands:

```
pip install numpy
```

```
pip install scipy (optional)
```

```
pip install matplotlib
```

```
pip install pandas
```

3 – NumPy Arrays

We can't do a lot of data science with NumPy alone. But it provides the basis for all the high-level libraries or modules for data science. It is essential for the efficient management of arrays and linear algebra.

In order to use NumPy, we of course have to import the respective module first.

```
import numpy as np
```

As you can see, we are also defining an *alias* here, so that we can address NumPy by just writing *np*.

Creating Arrays

To create a NumPy array, we just use the respective function *array* and pass a list to it.

```
a = np.array([10, 20, 30])
b = np.array([1, 77, 2, 3])
```

Now we can access the values in the same way as we would do it with a list.

```
print(a[0])
print(b[2])
```

Multi-Dimensional Arrays

The arrays we created are one-dimensional arrays. With NumPy, we can create large multi-dimensional arrays that have the same structure as a matrix.

```
a = np.array([
    [10, 20, 30],
    [40, 50, 60]
])
```

```
print(a)
```

Here, we pass two lists within a list as a parameter. This creates a 2x3 matrix. When we print the array, we get the following result:

```
[[10 20 30]
 [40 50 60]]
```

Since we now have two dimensions, we also need to address two indices, in order to access a specific element.

```
print(a[1][2])
```

In this case, we are addressing the second row (index one) and the third element or column (index two). Therefore, our result is *60*.

We can extend this principle as much as we want. For example, let's create a much bigger array.

```
a = np.array([
    [
        [10,20,30,40], [8,8,2,1], [1,1,1,2]
    ],
    [
        [9, 9, 2, 39], [1,2,3,3], [0,0,3,2]
    ],
    [
        [12,33,22,1], [22,1,22,2],
[0,2,3,1]
    ]
], dtype=float)
```

Here we have a 3x3x4 matrix and slowly but surely it becomes a bit irritating and we can't really grasp the structure of the array. This is especially the case when we get into four or more dimensions, since we only perceive three dimensions in everyday life.

You can imagine this three-dimensional array as a cube. We have three rows, four columns and three pages or layers. Such visualizations fail in higher dimensions.

Another thing that is worth mentioning is the parameter *dtype*. It stands for data type and allows us to specify which data type our values have. In this case we specified *float* and therefore our values will be stored as floating point numbers with the respective notation.

FILLING ARRAYS

Instead of manually filling our arrays with values, we can also use pre-defined functions in certain cases. The only thing we need to specify is the desired function and the shape of the array.

FULL FUNCTION

By using the *full* function for example, we fill an array of a certain shape with the same number. In this case we create a 3x5x4 matrix, which is filled with sevens.

```
a = np.full((3,5,4), 7)

print(a)
```

When we print it, we get the following output:

```
[[[7 7 7 7]
  [7 7 7 7]
  [7 7 7 7]]

 [[7 7 7 7]
  [7 7 7 7]
  [7 7 7 7]]]
```

ZEROS AND ONES

For the cases that we want arrays full of zeros or ones, we even have specific functions.

```
a = np.zeros((3,3))
b = np.ones((2,3,4,2))
```

Here we create a 3x3 array full of zeros and a four-dimensional array full of ones.

EMPTY AND RANDOM

Other options would be to create an empty array or one that is filled with random numbers. For this, we use the respective functions once again.

```
a = np.empty((4,4))
b = np.random.random((2,3))
```

The function *empty* creates an array without initializing the values at all. This makes it a little bit faster but also more dangerous to use, since the user needs to manually initialize all the values.

When using the *random* function, make sure that you are referring to the module *np.random*. You need to write it two times because otherwise you are calling the library.

RANGES

Instead of just filling arrays with the same values, we can fill create sequences of values by specifying the boundaries. For this, we can use two different functions, namely *arange and linspace*.

```
a = np.arange(10, 50, 5)
```

The function *arange* creates a list with values that range from the minimum to the maximum. The step-size has to be specified in the parameters.

```
[10 15 20 25 30 35 40 45]
```

In this example, we create have count from 10 to 45 by always adding 5. The result can be seen above.

By using *linspace* we also create a list from a minimum value to a maximum value. But instead of specifying the step-size, we specify the amount of values that we want to have in our list. They will all be spread evenly and have the same distance to their neighbors.

```
b = np.linspace(0, 100, 11)
```

Here, we want to create a list that ranges from 0 to 100 and contains 11 elements. This fits smoothly with a difference of 10 between all numbers. So the result looks like this:

```
[ 0.  10.  20.  30.  40.  50.  60.  70.  80.  90.
100.]
```

Of course, if we choose different parameters, the numbers don't be that "beautiful".

NOT A NUMBER (NAN)

There is a special value in NumPy that represents values that are not numbers. It is called *NaN* and stands for *Not a Number*. We basically just use it as a placeholder for empty spaces. It can be seen as a value that indicates that something is missing at that place.

When importing big data packets into our application, there will sometimes be missing data. Instead of just setting these values to zero or something else, we can set them to NaN and then filter these data sets out.

ATTRIBUTES OF ARRAYS

NumPy arrays have certain attributes that we can access and that provide information about the structure of it.

NUMPY ARRAY ATTRIBUTES	
ATTRIBUTE	**DESCRIPTION**
a.shape	Returns the shape of the array e.g. (3,3) or (3,4,7)
a.ndim	Returns how many dimensions our array has
a.size	Returns the amount of elements an array has
a.dtype	Returns the data type of the values in the array

MATHEMATICAL OPERATIONS

Now that we know how to create an array and what attributes it has, let's take a look at how to work with arrays. For this, we will start out with basic mathematical operations.

Arithmetic Operations

```
a = np.array([
    [1,4,2],
    [8,8,2]
])

print(a + 2)
print(a - 2)
print(a * 2)
print(a / 2)
```

When we perform basic arithmetic operations like addition, subtraction, multiplication and division to an array and a scalar, we apply the operation on every single element in the array. Let's take a look at the results:

```
[[ 3  6  4]
 [10 10  4]]
[[-1  2  0]
 [ 6  6  0]]
[[ 2  8  4]
 [16 16  4]]
[[0.5 2.  1. ]
 [4.  4.  1. ]]
```

As you can see, when we multiply the array by two, we multiply every single value in it by two. This is also the case for addition, subtraction and division. But what happens when we apply these operations on two arrays?

```
a = np.array([
    [1,4,2],
    [8,8,2]
])

b = np.array([
    [1,2,3]
])

c = np.array([
    [1],
    [2]
])

d = np.array([
    [1,2,3],
    [3,2,1]
])
```

In order to apply these operations on two arrays, we need to take care of the shapes. They don't have to be the same, but there has to be a reasonable way of performing the operations. We then again apply the operations on each element of the array.

For example, look at *a* and *b*. They have different shapes but when we add these two, they share at least the amount of columns.

```
print(a+b)
```

```
[[ 2  6  5]
 [ 9 10  5]]
```

Since they match the columns, we can just say that we add the individual columns, even if the amount of rows differs.

The same can also be done with *a* and *c* where the rows match and the columns differ.

```
print(a+c)
```

```
[[ 2  5  3]
 [10 10  4]]
```

And of course it also works, when the shapes match exactly. The only problem is when the shapes differ too much and there is no reasonable way of performing the operations. In these cases, we get *ValueErrors*.

MATHEMATICAL FUNCTIONS

Another thing that the NumPy module offers us is mathematical functions that we can apply to each value in an array.

NUMPY MATHEMATICAL FUNCTIONS	
FUNCTION	**DESCRIPTION**
np.exp(a)	Takes *e* to the power of each value
np.sin(a)	Returns the sine of each value
np.cos(a)	Returns the cosine of each value
np.tan(a)	Returns the tangent of each value
np.log(a)	Returns the logarithm of each value
np.sqrt(a)	Returns the square root of each value

AGGREGATE FUNCTIONS

Now we are getting into the statistics. NumPy offers us some so-called *aggregate functions* that we can use in order to get a key statistic from all of our values.

NUMPY AGGREGATE FUNCTIONS	
FUNCTION	**DESCRIPTION**
a.sum()	Returns the sum of all values in the array
a.min()	Returns the lowest value of the array
a.max()	Returns the highest value of the array
a.mean()	Returns the arithmetic mean of all values in the array
np.median(a)	Returns the median value of the array
np.std(a)	Returns the standard deviation of the values in the array

MANIPULATING ARRAYS

NumPy offers us numerous ways in which we can manipulate the data of our arrays. Here, we are going to take a quick look at the most important functions and categories of functions.

If you just want to change a single value however, you can just use the basic indexing of lists.

```
a = np.array([
    [4, 2, 9],
    [8, 3, 2]
])

a[1][2] = 7
```

SHAPE MANIPULATION FUNCTIONS

One of the most important and helpful types of functions are the *shape manipulating functions*. These allow us to restructure our arrays without changing their values.

SHAPE MANIPULATION FUNCTIONS	
FUNCTION	**DESCRIPTION**
a.reshape(x,y)	Returns an array with the same values structured in a different shape
a.flatten()	Returns a flattened one-dimensional copy of the array
a.ravel()	Does the same as *flatten* but works with the actual array instead of a copy
a.transpose()	Returns an array with the same values but swapped dimensions
a.swapaxes()	Returns an array with the same values but two swapped axes
a.flat	Not a function but an iterator for the flattened version of the array

There is one more element that is related to shape but it's not a function. It is called *flat* and it is an iterator for the flattened one-dimensional version of the array. *Flat* is not callable but we can iterate over it with *for* loops or index it.

```
for x in a.flat:
    print(x)

print(a.flat[5])
```

JOINING FUNCTIONS

We use *joining functions* when we combine multiple arrays into one new array.

JOINING FUNCTIONS	
FUNCTION	**DESCRIPTION**
np.concatenate(a,b)	Joins multiple arrays along an existing axis
np.stack(a,b)	Joins multiple arrays along a new axis
np.hstack(a,b)	Stacks the arrays horizontally (column-wise)
np.vstack(a,b)	Stacks the arrays vertically (row-wise)

In the following, you can see the difference between *concatenate* and *stack*:

```
a = np.array([10, 20, 30])
b = np.array([20, 20, 10])

print(np.concatenate((a,b)))
print(np.stack((a,b)))
```

```
[10 20 30 20 20 10]
[[10 20 30]
 [20 20 10]]
```

What *concatenate* does is, it joins the arrays together by just appending one onto the other. *Stack* on the other hand, creates an additional axis that separates the two initial arrays.

SPLITTING FUNCTIONS

We can not only join and combine arrays but also split them again. This is done by using *splitting functions* that split arrays into multiple sub-arrays.

SPLITTING FUNCTIONS	
FUNCTION	**DESCRIPTION**
np.split(a, x)	Splits one array into multiple arrays
np.hsplit(a, x)	Splits one array into multiple arrays horizontally (column-wise)
np.vsplit(a, x)	Splits one array into multiple arrays vertically (row-wise)

When splitting a list with the *split* function, we need to specify into how many sections we want to split our array.

```
a = np.array([
    [10, 20, 30],
    [40, 50, 60],
    [70, 80, 90],
    [100, 110, 120]
])

print(np.split(a, 2))
print(np.split(a, 4))
```

This array can be split into either two or four equally sized arrays on the default axis. The two possibilities are the following:

```
1: [[10, 20, 30],[40, 50, 60]]
2: [[70, 80, 90],[100, 110, 120]]
```

OR

```
1: [[10, 20, 30]]
2: [[40, 50, 60]]
3: [[70, 80, 90]]
4: [[100, 110, 120]]
```

ADDING AND REMOVING

The last manipulating functions that we are going to look at are the ones which allow us to *add* and to *remove* items.

ADDING AND REMOVING FUNCTIONS	
FUNCTION	**DESCRIPTION**
np.resize(a, (x,y))	Returns a resized version of the array and fills empty spaces by repeating copies of a
np.append(a, [...])	Appends values at the end of the array
np.insert(a, x, ...)	Insert a value at the index x of the array
np.delete(a, x, y)	Delete axes of the array

LOADING AND SAVING ARRAYS

Now last but not least, we are going to talk about loading and saving NumPy arrays. For this, we can use the integrated NumPy format or CSV-files.

NUMPY FORMAT

Basically, we are just serializing the object so that we can use it later. This is done by using the *save* function.

```
a = np.array([
    [10, 20, 30],
    [40, 50, 60],
    [70, 80, 90],
    [100, 110, 120]
])

np.save('myarray.npy', a)
```

Notice that you don't have to use the file ending *npy*. In this example, we just use it for clarity. You can pick whatever you want.

Now, in order to load the array into our script again, we will need the *load* function.

```
a = np.load('myarray.npy')
print(a)
```

CSV FORMAT

As I already mentioned, we can also save our NumPy arrays into CSV files, which are just comma-separated text files. For this, we use the function *savetxt*.

```
np.savetxt('myarray.csv', a)
```

Our array is now stored in a CSV-file which is very useful, because it can then also be read by other applications and scripts.

In order to read this CSV-file back into our script, we use the function *loadtxt*.

```
a = np.loadtxt('myarray.csv')
print(a)
```

If we want to read in a CSV-file that uses another separator than the default one, we can specify a certain delimiter.

```
a = np.loadtxt('myarray.csv',
delimiter=';')
print(a)
```

Now it uses semi-colons as separator when reading
the file. The same can also be done with the saving
or writing function.

4 – MATPLOTLIB DIAGRAMS

We have already mentioned that visualizing our data is crucial for data science. It gives us an overview and helps us to analyze data and make conclusions. Therefore, we will talk quite a lot about *Matplotlib*, the library which we use for plotting and visualizing.

PLOTTING MATHEMATICAL FUNCTIONS

Now, let's start out by drawing some mathematical functions first. In order to do so, we need to import the *matplotlib.pyplot* module and also NumPy.

```
import numpy as np
import matplotlib.pyplot as plt
```

Notice that we are also using an alias for *pyplot* here. In this case, it is *plt*.

In order to plot a function, we need the x-values or the input and the y-values or the output. So let us generate our x-values first.

```
x_values = np.linspace(0, 20, 100)
```

We are doing this by using the already known *linspace* function. Here we create an array with 100 values between 0 and 20. To now get our y-values, we just need to apply the respective function on our x-values. For this example, we are going with the sine function.

```
y_values = np.sin(x_values)
```

Remember that the function gets applied to every single item of the input array. So in this case, we have an array with the sine value of every element of the x-values array. We just need to plot them now.

```
plt.plot(x_values, y_values)
plt.show()
```

We do this by using the function *plot* and passing our x-values and y-values. At the end we call the *show* function, to display our plot.

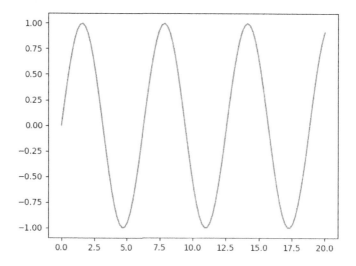

That was very simple. Now, we can go ahead and define our own function that we want to plot.

```
x = np.linspace(0, 10, 100)
y = (6 * x - 30) ** 2

plt.plot(x, y)
plt.show()
```

The result looks like this:

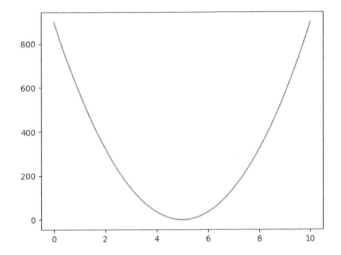

This is just the function $(6x - 30)^2$ plotted with Matplotlib.

VISUALIZING VALUES

What we can also do, instead of plotting functions, is just visualizing values in form of single dots for example.

```
numbers = 10 * np.random.random(100)

plt.plot(numbers, 'bo')
plt.show()
```

Here we are just generating 100 random numbers from 0 to 10. We then plot these numbers as blue dots. This is defined by the second parameter *'bo'*, where the first letter indicates the color (blue) and the second one the shape (dots). Here you can see what this looks like:

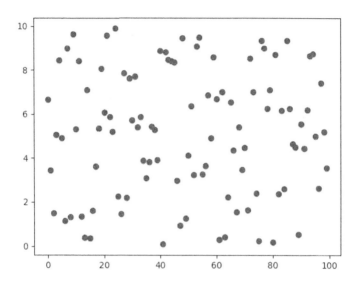

MULTIPLE GRAPHS

Our plots are not limited to only one single graph. We can plot multiple functions in different color and shape.

```
x = np.linspace(0,5,200)
y1 = 2 * x
y2 = x ** 2
y3 = np.log(x)

plt.plot(x, y1)
plt.plot(x, y2)
plt.plot(x, y3)
plt.show()
```

In this example, we first generate 200 x-values from 0 to 5. Then we define three different functions *y1, y2* and *y3*. We plot all these and view the plotting window. This is what it looks like:

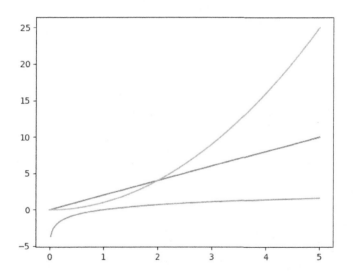

SUBPLOTS

Now, sometimes we want to draw multiple graphs but we don't want them in the same plot necessarily. For this reason, we have so-called *subplots*. These are plots that are shown in the same window but independently from each other.

```
x = np.linspace(0,5,200)
y1 = np.sin(x)
y2 = np.sqrt(x)

plt.subplot(211)
plt.plot(x, y1, 'r-')

plt.subplot(212)
plt.plot(x, y2, 'g--')

plt.show()
```

By using the function *subplot* we state that everything we plot now belongs to this specific subplot. The parameter we pass defines the grid of our window. The first digit indicates the number of rows, the second the number of columns and the last one the index of the subplot. So in this case, we have two rows and one column. Index one means that the respective subplot will be at the top.

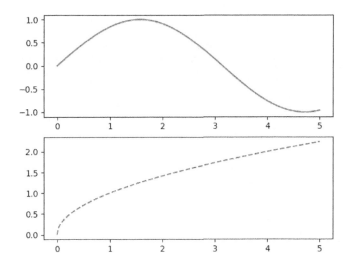

As you can see, we have two subplots in one window and both have a different color and shape. Notice that the ratios between the x-axis and the y-axis differ in the two plots.

MULTIPLE PLOTTING WINDOWS

Instead of plotting into subplots, we can also go ahead and plot our graphs into multiple windows. In Matplotlib we call these *figures*.

```
plt.figure(1)
plt.plot(x, y1, 'r-')

plt.figure(2)
plt.plot(x, y2, 'g--')
```

By doing this, we can show two windows with their graphs at the same time. Also, we can use subplots within figures.

PLOTTING STYLES

Matplotlib offers us many different plotting styles to choose from. If you are interested in how they look when they are applied, you can see an overview by going to the following website (I used a URL shortener to make it more readable):

https://bit.ly/2JfhJ4o

In order to use a style, we need to import the *style* module of Matplotlib and then call the function *use*.

```
from matplotlib import style

style.use('ggplot')
```

By using the *from ... import ...* notation we don't need to specify the parent module *matplotlib*. Here we apply the style of *ggplot*. This adds a grid and some other design changes to our plots. For more information, check out the link above.

LABELING DIAGRAMS

In order to make our graphs understandable, we need to label them properly. We should label the axes, we should give our windows titles and in some cases we should also add a legend.

SETTING TITLES

Let's start out by setting the titles of our graphs and windows.

```
x = np.linspace(0,50,100)
y = np.sin(x)

plt.title("Sine Function")
plt.suptitle("Data Science")
plt.grid(True)
plt.plot(x,y)

plt.show()
```

In this example, we used the two functions *title* and *suptitle*. The first function adds a simple title to our plot and the second one adds an additional centered title above it. Also, we used the *grid* function, to turn on the grid of our plot.

If you want to change the title of the window, you can use the *figure* function that we already know.

```
plt.figure("MyFigure")
```

LABELING AXES

As a next step, we are going to label our axes. For this, we use the two functions *xlabel* and *ylabel*.

```
plt.xlabel("x-values")
plt.ylabel("y-values")
```

You can choose whatever labels you like. When we combine all these pieces of code, we end up with a graph like this:

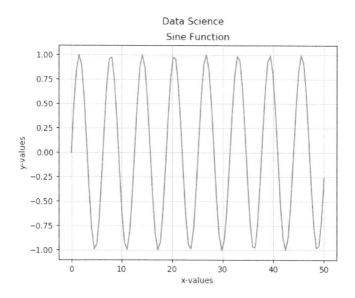

In this case, the labels aren't really necessary because it is obvious what we see here. But sometimes we want to describe what our values actually mean and what the plot is about.

LEGENDS

Sometimes we will have multiple graphs and objects in a plot. We then use legends to label these individual elements, in order to make everything more readable.

```
x = np.linspace(10,50,100)
y1 = np.sin(x)
y2 = np.cos(x)
y3 = np.log(x/3)

plt.plot(x,y1,'b-',label="Sine")
plt.plot(x,y2,'r-',label="Cosine")
plt.plot(x,y3,'g-',label="Logarithm")

plt.legend(loc='upper left')

plt.show()
```

Here we have three functions, *sine*, *cosine* and a *logarithmic* function. We draw all graphs into one plot and add a label to them. In order to make these labels visible, we then use the function *legend* and specify a location for it. Here we chose the *upper left*. Our result looks like this:

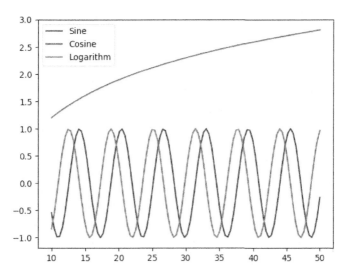

As you can see, the legend makes our plot way more readable and it also looks more professional.

SAVING DIAGRAMS

So now that we know quite a lot about plotting and graphing, let's take a look at how to save our diagrams.

```
plt.savefig("functions.png")
```

Actually, this is quite simple. We just plot whatever we want to plot and then use the function *savefig* to save our figure into an image file.

5 – Matplotlib Plot Types

In the last chapter, we mainly plotted functions and a couple of values. But Matplotlib offers a huge arsenal of different plot types. Here we are going to take a look at these.

Histograms

Let's start out with some statistics here. So-called *histograms* represent the distribution of numerical values. For example, we could graph the distribution of heights amongst students in a class.

```
mu, sigma = 172, 4
x = mu + sigma * np.random.randn(10000)
```

We start by defining a mean value *mu* (average height) and a standard deviation *sigma*. To create our x-values, we use our *mu* and *sigma* combined with 10000 randomly generated values. Notice that we are using the *randn* function here. This function generates values for a *standard normal distribution*, which means that we will get a bell curve of values.

```
plt.hist(x, 100, density=True, facecolor="blue")
```

Then we use the *hist* function, in order to plot our histogram. The second parameter states how many values we want to plot. Also, we want our values to be normed. So we set the parameter *density* to *True*. This means that our y-values will sum up to one and we can view them as percentages. Last but not least, we set the color to blue.

Now, when we show this plot, we will realize that it is a bit confusing. So we are going to add some labeling here.

```
plt.xlabel("Height")
plt.ylabel("Probability")
plt.title("Height of Students")
plt.text(160, 0.125,"μ = 172, σ = 4")
plt.axis([155,190,0,0.15])
plt.grid(True)
```

First we label the two axes. The x-values represent the height of the students, whereas the y-values represent the probability that a randomly picked student has the respective height. Besides the title, we also add some text to our graph. We place it at the x-value 160 and the y-value of 0.125. The text just states the values for μ (mu) and σ (sigma). Last but not least, we set the ranges for the two axes. Our x-values range from 155 to 190 and our y-values from 0 to 0.15. Also, the grid is turned on. This is what our graph looks like at the end:

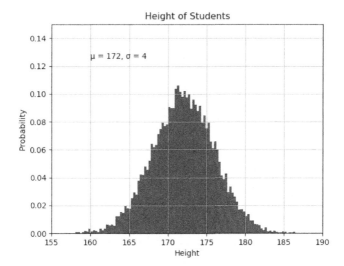

Height of Students

We can see the Gaussian bell curve which is typical for the standard normal distribution.

BAR CHART

For visualizing certain statistics, *bar charts* are oftentimes very useful, especially when it comes to categories. In our case, we are going to plot the skill levels of three different people in the IT realm.

```
bob = (90, 67, 87, 76)
charles = (80, 80, 47, 66)
daniel = (40, 95, 76, 89)

skills = ("Python", "Java", "Networking",
"Machine Learning")
```

Here we have the three persons *Bob, Charles* and *Daniel.* They are represented by tuples with four values that indicate their skill levels in Python programming, Java programming, networking and machine learning.

```
width = 0.2
index = np.arange(4)
plt.bar(index, bob,
        width=width, label="Bob")
plt.bar(index + width, charles,
        width=width, label="Charles")
plt.bar(index + width * 2, daniel,
        width=width, label="Daniel")
```

We then use the *bar* function to plot our bar chart. For this, we define an array with the indices one to four and a bar width of 0.2. For each person we plot the four respective values and label them.

```
plt.xticks(index + width, skills)
plt.ylim(0,120)
plt.title("IT Skill Levels")
plt.ylabel("Skill Level")
plt.xlabel("IT Skill")
plt.legend()
```

Then we label the x-ticks with the method *xticks* and set the limit of the y-axis to 120 to free up some space for our legend. After that we set a title and label the axes. The result looks like this:

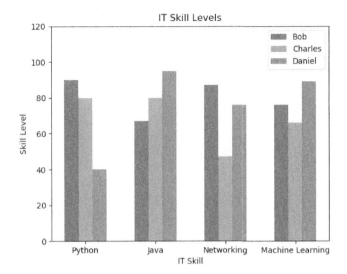

We can now see who is the most skilled in each category. Of course we could also change the graph so that we have the persons on the x-axis with the skill-colors in the legend.

PIE CHART

Pie charts are used to display proportions of numbers. For example, we could graph how many percent of the students have which nationality.

```
labels = ('American', 'German', 'French',
'Other')
values = (47, 23, 20, 10)
```

We have one tuple with our four nationalities. They will be our labels. And we also have one tuple with the percentages.

```
plt.pie(values,labels=labels,
        autopct="%.2f%%", shadow=True)
plt.title("Student Nationalities")

plt.show()
```

Now we just need to use the *pie* function, to draw our chart. We pass our values and our labels. Then we set the *autopct* parameter to our desired percentage format. Also, we turn on the *shadow* of the chart and set a title. And this is what we end up with:

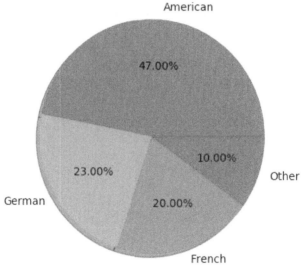

As you can see, this chart is perfect for visualizing percentages.

SCATTER PLOTS

So-called *scatter plots* are used to represent two-dimensional data using dots.

```
x = np.random.rand(50)
y = np.random.rand(50)

plt.scatter(x,y)

plt.show()
```

Here we just generate 50 random x-values and 50 random y-values. By using the *scatter* function, we can then plot them.

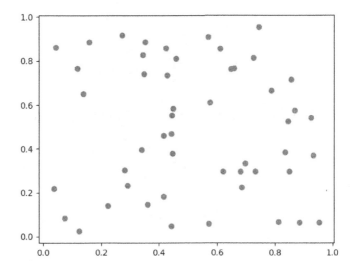

BOXPLOT

Boxplot diagrams are used, in order to split data into *quartiles*. We do that to get information about the distribution of our values. The question we want to answer is: How widely spread is the data in each of the quartiles.

```
mu, sigma = 172, 4
values = np.random.normal(mu,sigma,200)

plt.boxplot(values)
plt.title("Student's Height")
plt.ylabel("Height")
plt.show()
```

In this example, we again create a normal distribution of the heights of our students. Our mean value is 172, our standard deviation 4 and we generate 200 values. Then we plot our boxplot diagram.

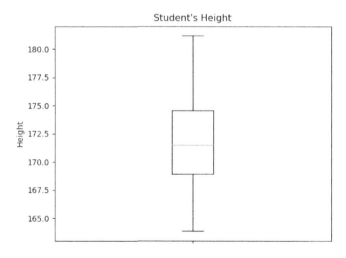

Here we see the result. Notice that a boxplot doesn't give information about the frequency of the individual values. It only gives information about the spread of the values in the individual quartiles. Every quartile has 25% of the values but some have a very small spread whereas others have quite a large one.

3D PLOTS

Now last but not least, let's take a look at 3D-plotting. For this, we will need to import another plotting module. It is called *mpl_toolkits* and it is part of the Matplotlib stack.

```
from mpl_toolkits import mplot3d
```

Specifically, we import the module *mplot3d* from this library. Then, we can use *3d* as a parameter when defining our axes.

```
ax = plt.axes(projection='3d')
plt.show()
```

We can only use this parameter, when *mplot3d* is imported. Now, our plot looks like this:

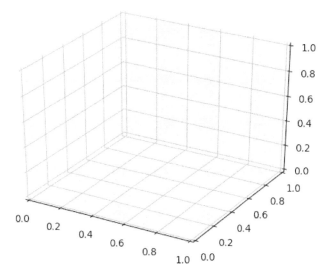

Since we are now plotting in three dimensions, we will also need to define three axes.

```
z = np.linspace(0, 20, 100)
x = np.sin(z)
y = np.cos(z)

ax = plt.axes(projection='3d')
ax.plot3D(x,y,z)
plt.show()
```

In this case, we are taking the z-axis as the input. The z-axis is the one which goes upwards. We define the x-axis and the y-axis to be a sine and cosine function. Then, we use the function *plot3D* to plot our function. We end up with this:

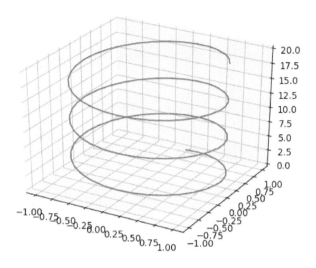

SURFACE PLOTS

Now in order to plot a function with a surface, we need to calculate every point on it. This is impossible, which is why we are just going to calculate enough to estimate the graph. In this case, x and y will be the input and the z-function will be the 3D-result which is composed of them.

```
ax = plt.axes(projection='3d')

def z_function(x, y):
    return np.sin(np.sqrt(x ** 2 + y ** 2))

x = np.linspace(-5, 5, 50)
y = np.linspace(-5, 5, 50)
```

We start by defining a *z_function* which is a combination of sine, square root and squaring the input. Our inputs are just 50 numbers from -5 to 5.

```
X, Y = np.meshgrid(x,y)
Z = z_function(X,Y)

ax.plot_surface(X,Y,Z)
plt.show()
```

Then we define new variables for x and y (we are using capitals this time). What we do is converting the x- and y-vectors into matrices using the *meshgrid* function. Finally, we use the *z_function* to calculate our z-values and then we plot our surface by using the method *plot_surface*. This is the result:

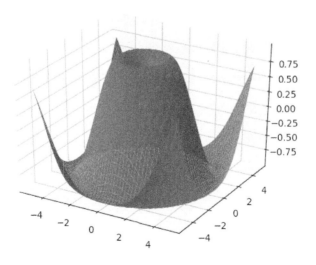

Play around with these charts and plots until you really understand them. Visualizing functions and data is very important in data science.

6 – PANDAS DATA ANALYSIS

Pandas is probably the most powerful libraries of this book. It provides high-performance tools for data manipulation and analysis. Furthermore, it is very effective at converting data formats and querying data out of databases. The two main data structures of Pandas are the *series* and the *data frame.* To work with Pandas, we need to import the module.

```
import pandas as pd
```

PANDAS SERIES

A series in Pandas is a one-dimensional array which is labeled. You can imagine it to be the data science equivalent of an ordinary Python dictionary.

```
series = pd.Series([10, 20, 30, 40],
                   ['A', 'B', 'C', 'D'])
```

In order to create a series, we use the constructor of the *Series* class. The first parameter that we pass is a list full of values (in this case numbers). The second parameter is the list of the indices or keys (in this case strings). When we now print our series, we can see what the structure looks like.

```
A    10
B    20
C    30
D    40
dtype: int64
```

The first column represents the indices, whereas the second column represents the actual values.

Accessing Values

The accessing of values works in the same way that it works with dictionaries. We need to address the respective index or key to get our desired value.

```
print(series['C'])
print(series[1])
```

As you can see, we can choose how we want to access our elements. We can either address the key or the position that the respective element is at.

Converting Dictionaries

Since series and dictionaries are quite similar, we can easily convert our Python dictionaries into Pandas series.

```
myDict = {'A':10, 'B':20, 'C':30}
series = pd.Series(myDict)
```

Now the keys are our indices and the values remain values. But what we can also do is, to change the order of the indices.

```
myDict = {'A':10, 'B':20, 'C':30}
series = pd.Series(myDict,
index=['C','A','B'])
```

Our series now looks like this:

```
C    30
A    10
B    20
dtype: int64
```

PANDAS DATA FRAME

In contrast to the series, a data frame is not one-dimensional but multi-dimensional and looks like a table. You can imagine it to be like an Excel table or a data base table.

```
data = {'Name': ['Anna', 'Bob', 'Charles'],
        'Age': [24, 32, 35],
        'Height': [176, 187, 175]}

df = pd.DataFrame(data)
```

To create a Pandas data frame, we use the constructor of the class. In this case, we first create a dictionary with some data about three persons. We feed that data into our data frame. It then looks like this:

```
       Name  Age  Height
0      Anna   24     176
1       Bob   32     187
2   Charles   35     175
```

As you can see, without any manual work, we already have a structured data frame and table.

To now access the values is a bit more complicated than with series. We have multiple columns and multiple rows, so we need to address two values.

```
print(df['Name'][1])
```

So first we choose the column *Name* and then we choose the second element (index one) of this column. In this case, this is *Bob*.

When we omit the last index, we can also select only the one column. This is useful when we want to save specific columns of our data frame into a new one. What we can also do in this case is to select multiple columns.

```
print(df[['Name', 'Height']])
```

Here we select two columns by addressing a list of two strings. The result is the following:

```
     Name   Height
0    Anna     176
1     Bob     187
2  Charles    175
```

DATA FRAME FUNCTIONS

Now, let us get a little bit more into the functions of a data frame.

BASIC FUNCTIONS AND ATTRIBUTES

For data frames we have a couple of basic functions and attributes that we already know from lists or NumPy arrays.

BASIC FUNCTIONS AND ATTRIBUTES	
FUNCTION	**DESCRIPTION**
df.T	Transposes the rows and columns of the data frame
df.dtypes	Returns data types of the data frame
df.ndim	Returns the number of dimensions of the data frame
df.shape	Returns the shape of the data frame
df.size	Returns the number of elements in the data frame
df.head(n)	Returns the first *n* rows of the data frame (default is five)
df.tail(n)	Returns the last *n* rows of the data frame (default is five)

STATISTICAL FUNCTIONS

For the statistical functions, we will now extend our data frame a little bit and add some more persons.

```
data = {'Name': ['Anna', 'Bob', 'Charles',
                 'Daniel', 'Evan', 'Fiona',
                 'Gerald', 'Henry',
'India'],
        'Age':
[24,32,35,45,22,54,55,43,25],
        'Height': [176,187,175,182,176,
                   189,165,187,167]}

df = pd.DataFrame(data)
```

STATISTICAL FUNCTIONS	
FUNCTION	**DESCRIPTION**
count()	Count the number of non-null elements
sum()	Returns the sum of values of the selected columns
mean()	Returns the arithmetic mean of values of the selected columns
median()	Returns the median of values of the selected columns
mode()	Returns the value that occurs most often in the columns selected
std()	Returns standard deviation of the values
min()	Returns the minimum value

max()	Returns the maximum value
abs()	Returns the absolute values of the elements
prod()	Returns the product of the selected elements
describe()	Returns data frame with all statistical values summarized

Now, we are not going to dig deep into every single function here. But let's take a look at how to apply some of them.

```
print(df['Age'].mean())
print(df['Height'].median())
```

Here we choose a column and then apply the statistical functions on it. What we get is just a single scalar with the desired value.

```
37.22222222222222
176.0
```

We can also apply the functions to the whole data frame. In this case, we get returned another data frame with the results for each column.

```
print(df.mean())
```

```
Age        37.222222
Height    178.222222
dtype: float64
```

Applying Numpy Functions

Instead of using the built-in Pandas functions, we can also use the methods we already know. For this, we just use the *apply* function of the data frame and then pass our desired method.

```
print(df['Age'].apply(np.sin))
```

In this example, we apply the sine function onto our ages. It doesn't make any sense but it demonstrates how this works.

Lambda Expressions

A very powerful in Python are *lambda expression*. They can be thought of as nameless functions that we pass as a parameter.

```
print(df['Age'].apply(lambda x: x * 100))
```

By using the keyword *lambda* we create a temporary variable that represents the individual values that we are applying the operation onto. After the colon, we define what we want to do. In this case, we multiply all values of the column *Age* by 100.

```
df = df[['Age', 'Height']]

print(df.apply(lambda x: x.max() -
x.min()))
```

Here we removed the *Name* column, so that we only have numerical values. Since we are applying our expression on the whole data frame now, *x* refers to the whole columns. What we do here is calculating the difference between the maximum value and the minimum value.

```
Age        33
Height     24
dtype: int64
```

The oldest and the youngest are 33 years apart and the tallest and the tiniest are 24 centimeters apart.

ITERATING

Iterating over data frames is quite easy with Pandas. We can either do it in the classic way or use specific functions for it.

```
for x in df['Age']:
    print(x)
```

As you can see, iterating over a column's value is very simple and nothing new. This would print all the ages. When we iterate over the whole data frame, our control variable takes on the column names.

STATISTICAL FUNCTIONS	
FUNCTION	**DESCRIPTION**
iteritems()	Iterator for key-value pairs
iterrows()	Iterator for the rows (index, series)
itertuples()	Iterator for the rows as named tuples

Let's take a look at some practical examples.

```
for key, value in df.iteritems():
    print("{}: {}".format(key, value))
```

Here we use the *iteritems* function to iterate over key-value pairs. What we get is a huge output of all rows for each column.

On the other hand, when we use *iterrows*, we can print out all the column-values for each row or index.

```
for index, value in df.iterrows():
    print(index,value)
```

We get packages like this one for every index:

```
0 Name        Anna
Age           24
Height       176
Name: 0, dtype: object
```

SORTING

One very powerful thing about Pandas data frames is that we can easily sort them.

SORT BY INDEX

```
df = pd.DataFrame(np.random.rand(10,2),

index=[1,5,3,6,7,2,8,9,0,4],
                    columns=['A','B'])
```

Here we create a new data frame, which is filled with random numbers. We specify our own indices and as you can see, they are completely unordered.

```
print(df.sort_index())
```

By using the method *sort_index*, we sort the whole data frame by the index column. The result is now sorted:

```
          A          B
0   0.193432   0.514303
1   0.391481   0.193495
2   0.159516   0.607314
3   0.273120   0.056247

...       ...        ...
```

INPLACE PARAMETER

When we use functions that manipulate our data frame, we don't actually change it but we return a manipulated copy. If we wanted to apply the changes on the actual data frame, we would need to do it like this:

```
df = df.sort_index()
```

But Pandas offers us another alternative as well. This alternative is the parameter *inplace*. When this parameter is set to *True*, the changes get applied to our actual data frame.

```
df.sort_index(inplace=True)
```

SORT BY COLUMNS

Now, we can also sort our data frame by specific columns.

```
data = {'Name': ['Anna', 'Bob', 'Charles',
                 'Daniel', 'Evan', 'Fiona',
                 'Gerald', 'Henry',
'India'],
        'Age':
[24,24,35,45,22,54,54,43,25],
        'Height': [176,187,175,182,176,
                   189,165,187,167]}

df = pd.DataFrame(data)

df.sort_values(by=['Age', 'Height'],
               inplace=True)

print(df)
```

Here we have our old data frame slightly modified. We use the function *sort_values* to sort our data frames. The parameter *by* states the columns that we are sorting by. In this case, we are first sorting by age and if two persons have the same age, we sort by height.

JOINING AND MERGING

Another powerful concept in Pandas is *joining* and *merging* data frames.

```
names = pd.DataFrame({
    'id': [1,2,3,4,5],
    'name': ['Anna', 'Bob', 'Charles',
             'Daniel', 'Evan'],
})

ages = pd.DataFrame({
    'id': [1,2,3,4,5],
    'age': [20,30,40,50,60]
})
```

Now when we have two separate data frames which are related to one another, we can combine them into one data frame. It is important that we have a common column that we can merge on. In this case, this is *id*.

```
df = pd.merge(names,ages,on='id')
df.set_index('id', inplace=True)
```

First we use the method *merge* and specify the column to merge on. We then have a new data frame with the combined data but we also want our *id* column to be the index. For this, we use the *set_index* method.

The result looks like this:

```
     name  age
id
1     Anna   20
2      Bob   30
3  Charles   40
4   Daniel   50
5     Evan   60
```

JOINS

It is not necessarily always obvious *how* we want to merge our data frames. This is where *joins* come into play. We have four types of joins.

JOIN MERGE TYPES	
JOIN	**DESCRIPTION**
left	Uses all keys from left object and merges with right
right	Uses all keys from right object and merges with left
outer	Uses all keys from both objects and merges them
inner	Uses only the keys which both objects have and merges them (default)

Now let's change our two data frames a little bit.

```
names = pd.DataFrame({
    'id': [1,2,3,4,5,6],
    'name': ['Anna', 'Bob', 'Charles',
             'Daniel', 'Evan', 'Fiona'],
})
```

```
ages = pd.DataFrame({
    'id': [1,2,3,4,5,7],
    'age': [20,30,40,50,60,70]
})
```

Our *names* frame now has an additional index *6* and an additional name. And our *ages* frame has an additional index *7* with an additional name.

```
df = pd.merge(names,ages,on='id',
how='inner')
df.set_index('id', inplace=True)
```

If we now perform the default *inner join*, we will end up with the same data frame as in the beginning. We only take the keys which both objects have. This means one to five.

```
df = pd.merge(names,ages,on='id',
how='left')
df.set_index('id', inplace=True)
```

When we use the *left join*, we get all the keys from the *names* data frame but not the additional index 7 from ages. This also means that *Fiona* won't be assigned any age.

```
        name    age
id
1       Anna    20.0
2        Bob    30.0
3    Charles    40.0
4     Daniel    50.0
5       Evan    60.0
6      Fiona    NaN
```

The same principle goes for the *right join* just the other way around.

```
df = pd.merge(names,ages,on='id',
how='right')
df.set_index('id', inplace=True)
```

```
        name  age
id
1       Anna   20
2        Bob   30
3    Charles   40
4     Daniel   50
5       Evan   60
7        NaN   70
```

Now, we only have the keys from the *ages* frame and the *6* is missing. Finally, if we use the *outer join*, we combine all keys into one data frame.

```
df = pd.merge(names,ages,on='id',
how='outer')
df.set_index('id', inplace=True)
```

```
        name   age
id
1       Anna  20.0
2        Bob  30.0
3    Charles  40.0
4     Daniel  50.0
5       Evan  60.0
6      Fiona   NaN
7        NaN  70.0
```

QUERYING DATA

Like in databases with SQL, we can also query data from our data frames in Pandas. For this, we use the function *loc*, in which we put our expression.

```
print(df.loc[df['Age'] == 24])
print(df.loc[(df['Age'] == 24) &
            (df['Height'] > 180)])
print(df.loc[df['Age'] > 30]['Name'])
```

Here we have some good examples to explain how this works. The first expression returns all rows where the value for *Age* is 24.

```
   Name  Age  Height
0  Anna   24     176
1   Bob   24     187
```

The second query is a bit more complicated. Here we combine two conditions. The first one is that the age needs to be 24 but we then combine this with the condition that the height is greater than 180. This leaves us with one row.

```
   Name  Age  Height
1   Bob   24     187
```

In the last expression, we can see that we are only choosing one column to be returned. We want the names of all people that are older than 30.

```
2    Charles
3     Daniel
5      Fiona
6     Gerald
7      Henry
```

READ DATA FROM FILES

Similar to NumPy, we can also easily read data from external files into Pandas. Let's say we have an CSV-File like this (opened in Excel):

▲	A	B	C	D
1	id	name	age	height
2	1	Anna	20	178
3	2	Bob	30	172
4	3	Charles	40	189
5	4	Daniel	50	192
6	5	Evan	60	183
7	6	Fiona	70	165
8				

The only thing that we need to do now is to use the function *read_csv* to import our data into a data frame.

```
df = pd.read_csv('data.csv')
df.set_index('id', inplace=True)
print(df)
```

We also set the index to the *id* column again. This is what we have imported:

```
        name  age  height
id
1       Anna   20     178
2        Bob   30     172
3    Charles   40     189
4     Daniel   50     192
5       Evan   60     183
6      Fiona   70     165
```

This of course, also works the other way around. By using the method *to_csv*, we can also save our data frame into a CSV-file.

```
data = {'Name': ['Anna', 'Bob', 'Charles',
                 'Daniel', 'Evan', 'Fiona',
                 'Gerald', 'Henry',
'India'],
        'Age':
[24,24,35,45,22,54,54,43,25],
        'Height': [176,187,175,182,176,
                   189,165,187,167]}

df = pd.DataFrame(data)
df.to_csv('mydf.csv')
```

Then we have this CSV-file (opened in Excel):

	A	B	C	D
1		Name	Age	Height
2	0	Anna	24	176
3	1	Bob	24	187
4	2	Charles	35	175
5	3	Daniel	45	182
6	4	Evan	22	176
7	5	Fiona	54	189
8	6	Gerald	54	165
9	7	Henry	43	187
10	8	India	25	167
11				

PLOTTING DATA

Since Pandas builds on Matplotlib, we can easily visualize the data from our data frame.

```
data = {'Name': ['Anna', 'Bob', 'Charles',
                 'Daniel', 'Evan', 'Fiona',
                 'Gerald', 'Henry',
'India'],
        'Age':
[24,24,35,45,22,54,54,43,25],
        'Height': [176,187,175,182,176,
                   189,165,187,167]}

df = pd.DataFrame(data)
df.sort_values(by=['Age', 'Height'])
df.hist()
plt.show()
```

In this example, we use the method *hist* to plot a histogram of our numerical columns. Without specifying anything more, this is what we end up with:

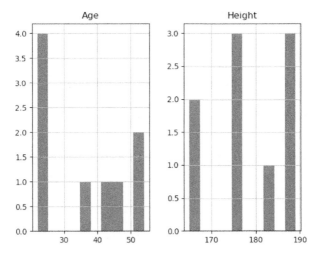

But we can also just use the function *plot* to plot our data frame or individual columns.

```
df.plot()
plt.show()
```

The result is the following:

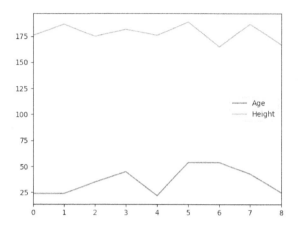

Of course we can also just use the Matplotlib library itself and pass the columns as parameters.

```
plt.plot(df['Age'], 'bo')
plt.show()
```

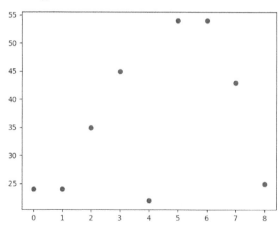

WHAT'S NEXT?

Finally, we are done with the third volume of the Python Bible series. It was very practical and went deep into the topic of data science. This has now laid the foundation for more complex topics like machine learning and finance, which will be the follow-ups to this book. You are on a very good path! Just make sure you practice everything until you really understand the material that we talked about.

You are now definitely able to find some huge data sets online (maybe in CSV-format) and analyze them with Python. And I encourage you to do that. We only learn by doing and practicing. In the next volumes we will also import data from online sources and APIs. And we are not only going to analyze this data but also to make predictions with it.

Now that you've read the first three volumes of this series, I encourage you to continue on this journey because it is NOW that things get really interesting. I hope you could get some value out of this book and that it helped you to become a better programmer. So stay tuned and read the next volume, which is about machine learning!

Also, if you are interested in free educational content about programming and machine learning, check out https://www.neuralnine.com/

Last but not least, a little reminder. This book was written for you, so that you can get as much value as possible and learn to code effectively. If you find this book valuable or you think you learned something new, please write a quick review on Amazon. It is completely free and takes about one minute. But it helps me produce more high quality books, which you can benefit from.

Thank you!

NeuralNine

If you are interested in free educational content about programming and machine learning, check out https://www.neuralnine.com/

There we have free blog posts, videos and more for you! Also, you can follow the ***@neuralnine*** Instagram account for daily infographics about programming and AI!

Website: https://www.neuralnine.com/

Instagram: @neuralnine

YouTube: NeuralNine

Printed in Great Britain
by Amazon